The Crucified Couple!

Success Through Sacrifice in Relationships

I have been crucified with Christ and I no longer live, but Christ lives in me. The life I now live in the body, I live by faith in the Son of God, who loved me and gave himself for me (Galatians 2:20).

Pastor Joel L. Rissinger
11/12/2014

All rights reserved. No part of this publication may be reproduced or transmitted for commercial purposes, except for brief quotations in printed reviews, without written permission of the author.

Unless otherwise indicated, Scripture quotations are taken from the HOLY BIBLE, NEW INTERNATIONAL VERSION®. NIV®. Copyright © 1973, 1978, 1984 by Biblica, Inc.™ Used by permission of Zondervan. All rights reserved worldwide, www.zondervan.com or by the Holy Bible, Holman Christian Standard Version ® Copyright © 2204 by B&H Publishing, Inc. TM Used by permission of B&H Publishing. All rights reserved worldwide, www. Hcsb.org.

This book provides frank and honest advice about the necessity of dying to self to live for God. Couples who embrace this will succeed. Those who do not, will likely fail!

Endorsements

"It would be enough to learn from a pastor who has helped hundreds of couples navigate marriage, but it is especially engaging when he takes us back to the Cross of Christ. Putting another's interests ahead of your own on a consistent basis for many years is extraordinary and Joel joins the Apostle Paul in sharing that 'our attitude should be the same as that of Christ, while being in nature, God, did not consider equality with God something to be grasped, but made himself nothing, taking the very nature of a servant.' Philippians 2:5-6." **Brian Doyle, President, Iron Sharpens Iron**

"Speaking just as frank & honest as in his previous excellent book, The Crucified Church, author & Pastor Joel Rissinger again continues along the same track in this outstanding follow up, only this time Joel leads us to a long overdue funeral needed in each Christian once again everywhere, the 'death' of self.

Joel leads a loud & clear clarion call desperately needed in the Body of Christ at this hour, that to serve Man, is in effect to serve God." -- **Rev. Al Stewart, DD., Pastor, Forest Community Church, Forest, Va.**

*"Learning how to implement Biblical truth shows us how wisely live our lives. Pastor Joel Rissinger not only teaches truth about how to have a fulfilling marriage; but he does it in a way that is practical, interesting and insightful. Read "The Crucified Couple" and be reminded that your marriage can reflect God's love and lead to great joy!"--***Dr. Brent Allen, District Executive Minister, Converge Northeast**

Marriage is not a 50/50 commitment as many people teach. Pastor Joel Rissinger is right on target with "The Crucified Couple!" The subtitle says it all: "Living Sacrificially as one...for Christ." When each spouse gives 100%, even as Christ gave and expects His Church to give, there is a healthy and Christ-honoring marriage that reflects the eternal relationship we have as followers of Jesus. I hope to use this book with every couple who comes to me for premarital and marital counseling.--

Dr. Roger D. Haber, Adjunct Staff Conflict Response Minister, The American Baptist Churches of Massachusetts

"Joel Rissinger knows what it takes to live a Godly marriage - taking this sacred relationship to the cross! He poignantly lays out a beautiful plan to build or rebuild a marriage. From communication to sex and budgets, Pastor Joel teaches us all the anointed power of a crucified marriage that results in more than a happy marriage - but in truly glorifying God through His perfect relational plan." **Dr. Jim Harris, Author of 14 books including "Our Unfair Advantage: How to Unleash the Power of the Holy Spirit in Your Business."**

To my wife Karen—you are a blessing from God and, for me, the perfect model of what Jesus wants for all of us, his Bride, the Church.

To my son David—my firstborn, intelligent beyond your years. Thank you for your love and constant challenge to keep me honest and on track.

To my daughter Shelly—my baby girl, who's not a baby anymore, but has one of her own. You're a great daughter, wife, and Mommy. Your love of Jesus and willingness to risk all to share Him makes me more proud than you'll ever know.

To Alex, my son-in-law. You've provided the greatest gift a Dad could ever desire: someone who really loves, cares for, and values his baby girl. I'm proud to call you son.

To Aadi—my precious granddaughter. My prayer is that this book someday helps you and your future husband. Not sure if I'll be around to witness your wedding and help you get off to a good start in person...but I pray this book will help you nonetheless. Love you baby!

To the elders, leaders, and much-loved members of Mill Pond Church. You are the best spiritual family I could ever dream of or imagine. Thanks for the honor of being your pastor!

To so many fellow pastors and leaders who have encouraged me and given me support for this work...thank you so much! I'm blessed to have friends like you!

Index

Intro……………………………………………………page 8

CHAPTER ONE: The Death of Death to Self……………page 15

CHAPTER TWO: The Key to Marriage—Sacrifice………page 27

CHAPTER THREE: Sacrificial Communication…………page 31

CHAPTER FOUR: Sacrificial Conflict Resolution………page 67

CHAPTER FIVE: Dying to your budget…………………page 78

CHAPTER SIX: Sacrificial Sex……………………………..page 83

CHAPTER SEVEN: Crucified Fun Times…………………..page 88

CHAPTER EIGHT: Family and Friends…letting go!……..page 96

CHAPTER NINE: Is sacrifice enabling?…………………….page 105

CHAPTER TEN: Defining Success………………………page 110

CHAPTER ELEVEN: Separation and Divorce.,,,,,,,,,,,,,,,,page 116

CHAPTER TWELVE: Getting Help…………………… page 124

Appendix:
    Discussion Questions for Couples/Small Groups..page 130
    Recommended Reading………………………….page 137
    Sample Family Budget……..………………….page 138
    Footnotes………………………………………….page 139
    Recommended Reading………………………….page 141
    About the Author………………………………….page 142

The Crucified Couple, Living sacrificially as one, for Christ.

By Pastor Joel L. Rissinger, MA

Intro

"I just want to be happy Pastor," Bob said, "Is that so much to ask? I want basic things—sex, an encouraging word now and then, and some peace when I come home without all that nag-nag-nagging!" "Pastor," Paula responded, "he NEVER wants to talk! When he does talk, why is it always about him? Why doesn't he ever listen? Can't he show that he cares—even a little bit—about ME?"

Sound familiar?

It should. To one degree or another, this conversation is repeated a thousand times a day by couples of every demographic distinction imaginable. Old, young, black-white-Asian-or Hispanic, all are susceptible and most fall into this pattern at least in part. She feels unloved and he feels disrespected and harassed. The specifics vary, but the general needs do not.

To combat this, over the last 25 years of ministry I've counseled, taught, and encouraged hundreds of couples. I've seen long-time, married couples succeed and fail. I've watched new, soon-to-be-wed couples with "stars in their eyes" who made marriage work and I've seen some burn out and quit after just a few months. I've read books, gone to seminars, given and received countless hours of training in marriage, couples counseling, personality assessment and more. I've enjoyed retreats in nice hotels and in rustic camp settings and sent couples to these and other venues—all with a "hit and miss" track record of success…

Why?

Why, despite our best efforts to help and train, do some couples make it while others do not? Why despite all the powerful and inspirational teaching offered by groups like Promise Keepers, Iron Sharpens Iron, Women of Faith, Knights of the 21st Century, and many more—does the divorce rate still hover at around 50% both in and outside of the Christian Church?1

Why?

I think the answer is simple…it's because we've forgotten the most basic teaching of our faith. We've neglected to apply the very core of Christian doctrine to the most basic of institutions, marriage. Notice the connection the Apostle Paul makes between this doctrine and our own existence as followers of Christ,

> *"I have been crucified with Christ and I no longer live, but Christ lives in me. The life I now live in the flesh, I live by faith in the Son of God who loved me and gave Himself for me (Gal. 2:20, HCSB)."*

Submitting to one another in the fear of Christ…Wives submit to your own husbands as to the Lord…Husbands love your wives just as also Christ loved the church and gave Himself for her… (Eph. 5:21, 22, and 25, HCSB)."

The Cross is the foundational distinctive that makes Christianity both unique and life-changing as compared to all other world religions. Nothing is more drastic and distinctive than God dying for people. God, giving up His superior position to become like us such that he could suffer, die, and become the cleansing sacrifice for all sin. Paul says he was "crucified with Christ." Elsewhere he speaks of being a new creation, a new person alive in Christ with a new identity…literally dead to self—the old man—and alive to and through Jesus Christ!

Somewhere along the way, even Christians and Churches have forgotten the personal, familial, and societal impact of the Cross. We've turned to pop-psychology as our savior and believed that the key to success and happiness isn't found in crucifixion or sacrifice, but in pursuit of our own spiritual, emotional, and physical desires. We believe, at least subconsciously, that if we pursue the right person and win them over, (maybe even going so far as to suggest that God has picked him/her for us by fiat and we simply have to find the soul mate He's predestined for us), we will be blissfully happy all the days of our lives! We think that the job of our spouse is to make us happy and, if we find "the right one," he/she undoubtedly WILL!

How's that working out for us?

Horribly! I won't quote statistics because you don't need them. You are likely to have come from a divorced/broken family situation or been in one yourself. If not, (Praise God), you no doubt know people intimately who have been impacted by divorce. From these experiences, you've seen what doesn't work—the unending pursuit of personal satisfaction!

Even when we expound Paul's brilliantly inspired marriage text in Ephesians 5, we tend to focus either on rote obedience to the marching orders given to husbands and wives or the benefit of being loved and/or respected. What we MISS all too often is the miraculous synergy that occurs when a man or a woman sacrifices their primary sense of desire for the needs of their partner.

Could it be that Jesus actually knew what he was talking about when he said,

> *"Give and it will be given to you; a good measure—pressed down, shaken together and running over—will be poured into your lap. For with the measure you use, it will be measured back to you (Luke 6:38, HCSB)."*

Could it be that Jesus—author and finisher of our faith, Creator of all, God—Lord—King—and Savior of all mankind—could it be that He is telling the truth? Could it be that despite an offended spouse's seeming inability to respond, an angry spouse's unwillingness to be kind, etc.; could it be that God has created a supernatural law of the universe PROMISING blessing when we give?

I'm no scholar, but yes, that's what the text says to me!

So how did we go from what I call, "give-living" and sacrificial relationships to the selfish pursuit of happiness at all costs? If selfishness is at the root of our self-destruction as couples, shouldn't we try to understand how we got to this point and then do what we can to reverse it?

That my friends, is the focus of this book...

Chapter One: The Death of Death to Self…

A pastor I knew used to love to tell people that there are two basic ways of life: give and get. I would add that there are two basic views of human beings: good and bad. Ironically, those who view people as basically good are probably more likely to encourage and live the "get way," while those who see people as innately corrupt/bad will likely live the "give way."

This is logical in that if I think I'm basically "good," then what I want must be "good" too. So to pursue/take it is natural and appropriate. Thus, I live the "get" way. On the other hand, if I think that my nature is sinful and thus, "bad," I'm less likely to pursue taking/getting everything that nature craves. Instead, I'm more apt to follow the example of Jesus—giving and "laying down (my) life" for those around me (1 John 3:16).

Popular Psychology, and sadly much of what passes for Christian Counseling, is based on the idea that people are basically good. The assumption is that everyone wants what is good and will do what's good if their hurts, hang-ups, and false beliefs are removed. We encourage people to love themselves more and thus, albeit inadvertently, encourage them to be quite selfish.

A biblical worldview starts with the idea that man is NOT innately "good," but since the fall, actually evil. Jeremiah wrote that the "heart" or inner man is deceitfully evil—so "desperately wicked" that nobody but God can really understand it (Jer. 17:9-10). Biblically, the answer to this problem is a new heart created when Jesus lives in that person through the person of the Holy Spirit. Then, and only then, can that person choose to walk by the spirit and not by the basic, selfish desires that are part of our human, fallen sin nature.

So with such a vast, literally polar-opposite perspective, how did 21st Century culture arrive at a point where the dominant view is that man is good and what he wants is also good? While detailed, the answer is in essence simple. The post-enlightenment move toward Darwinism as a basic premise for education, business, social structure, etc.; inevitably led to this change. Once we put God aside as our first cause and ultimate guide, we were left with ourselves. If survival of the fittest and natural selection led us to our modern state, it must be good…and so must we be good as well.

Put another way, if I believe that my natural motivation is to survive and that this is evolution's way of making sure both I and my species thrive, then my natural motivation is good. If they're good for me and I'm a man, than they must also be good for mankind. Furthermore, if there is no God, I am the ultimate source of morality. I decide what is true, right, and just for me. Collectively, society decides what is good for itself, but if I disagree, I leave that social system and find another because I am right (too). And, since I determine what is good, I must be good. Therefore, what I want is good (for survival of the fittest), and I am good (since self-preservation ensures a positive outcome under natural selection).

If I believe in God and that the Bible is His revelation to man, I see things quite differently. First, I see God as the source of morality over myself or anyone else. I see God as good. Next, I come to see that my natural state is a fallen one, thus opposed to God who is good. Therefore, I see that my desires and motivations are often evil, not good and should be subject to God's revealed will. I literally check myself daily to be sure I'm moving closer to God's glorious ideal and away from my own selfish desires.

Not only are there vast differences in the philosophical tenants of these worldviews, these two views of human nature and behavior lead to very different paths—especially with regard to marriage and relationships. One sees marriage as a place to achieve ultimate personal satisfaction emotionally, sexually, relationally, and spiritually. With this worldview, one's spouse is a source of friendship, sexual pleasure, partnership for greater achievement in life, etc. The goal with this approach is to find that person—the one more likely to provide these things and then do what one has to in order to secure that person as a marriage partner and then maintain that relationship for the purposes of self-actualization.

The biblical view of marriage is quite different. People who view life through this paradigm see marriage first and foremost as a way to reflect the image and glory of God (See Gen. 1:26, 2:24, etc.). While marriage provides partnership, companionship, sexual pleasure, family, and more—the focus is to learn to give and surrender the "self" just as Christ did for his bride, the Church (Eph. 5:21-33). When problems arise in this marriage, the presumption is that change is needed—not just in one's partner, but in oneself!

How did we get to the point where what once was the norm—a biblical view of self—has been replaced by a more secular, selfish view? Darwinism, the rise of Secular Humanism, and other philosophies have overtaken the teaching of biblical values at school, at home, and even at church. This wasn't difficult—it's certainly easier to tell people that they are good than to say they are evil. Telling people they need to change isn't as popular as telling them they should "come" (and remain) "just as (they) are." Ultimately, society "opted" for an atheistic view of cosmology because it's attractive to believe that we can choose our own morality and values in lieu of having God tell us what to do. This works—if we believe that we're good and these moral choices are thus, good as well.

We shouldn't gloss-over this point. The "Big Bang Theory" as it's often called, gives us god without a brain and thus no moral authority. Every divine attribute is acknowledged in this theory but instead of ascribing these traits to God, we assign them to a tiny pin-point of compressed matter and energy. We say that pin-point–sized spec blew up and generated all the energy in the universe, thus we say it's omnipotent. We say this dust spec was always there—it had no origin and was thus eternal and self-existent. We say it scattered after the "bang" such that all matter in the known universe came from this spec—thus it's omnipresent. Omnipotence, omnipresence, self-existence, etc., are divine traits—attributes of God. So we've made this speck of dust into a god. The only thing it lacks is intelligence.

So why would we subscribe to a theory with a mindless god?

Because if we give god a philosophical lobotomy, he can't tell us what to do. Again, we are then left with ourselves as the supreme moral authority. Anyone who challenges this and suggests that there is an intelligent first cause—a literal, personal God who has moral authority—anyone with THAT conviction is considered dangerous, at best.

Sadly, this perspective has even crept subtly into the modern church.

I've often joked about this. Imagine the Apostle Paul who referred to Cretans as fat liars (Titus 1:12) or Jesus who opened one public presentation by calling his audience a bunch of snakes (Matt. 23:33), applying for a job as pastor of a modern American Protestant Church. Would either of them have a snowball's chance in Hades of making it past the first round of interviews? How about John the Baptist? Peter? James? None of them was known for being politically correct or even overly-sensitive to people's self- esteem. I'm not saying that these men were hateful or mean—what I'm saying is that their solution to the sin and trouble in people's lives was NOT to tell them how wonderful they were!

Sadly, the 21st Century Church has a "better" plan. We DO tell people that they are good and just need Jesus' help to be great. Our paradigm has shifted and the fruits are not so good. In brief, we've stopped living sacrificially. After all, if something is good, why put it to death? If my basic nature, inner man, or "heart" is good—I should keep it as is, not change it. This approach has allowed us to avoid the dichotomy of Jesus' life and teachings. He told us to give if we wanted to receive. He told us the meek inherit the earth. He said if we seek to save our life, we'll lose it and vise- versa. He told us to "take up (our) cross" and follow him. All of this goes out the proverbial window if we embrace the idea that we're basically good and we should pursue our desires because they too are basically good.

This mentality impacts everything—not just marriage. Politicians, even supposed "Christian" ones, clearly pursue more and more power and money in lieu of true servant leadership. Corporate executives, union bosses, and workers have one thing in common—greed! Our belief is that we MUST "take care of number one," because if we don't, nobody else will. We fail to recognize God in this process or Jesus' promise that if we sought his Kingdom first, all our true needs, (perhaps not "wants"), would nonetheless be taken care of by Him (Matt. 6:33).

So we enter marriage ill-equipped for success. We think the entire key to happiness is to find our "soul mate," that one predestined soul who will make us happy by giving us what we need. We know WE are basically good and our desires are too. Thus, we clearly expect the other person to like us and fulfill those desires. When, (not if), they don't, we simply discard them like a used tissue and move on to the next—hoping "this time will be different," because obviously "this time" we're marrying a different person. The REAL problem, our sinful self, remains unchanged. We become like the old saying regarding church-hoppers. We tell them, "If you find the perfect church, don't join it because it won't be perfect anymore." We SHOULD say, "If you find the perfect fiancé, don't marry that person because they won't be perfect any longer."

Even couples who "stick with it" and refuse to divorce are often sadly miserable due to this flawed premise. As a pastor deeply involved with marriage counseling and preparation for more than 25 years, I wish I had a proverbial dollar for every time a husband has complained to me about feeling disrespected or "hen-pecked." I'd be equally as rich if I collected from every wife who has told me that she felt unloved, uncherished, or unappreciated (See Eph. 5:33). What's sad is that when I explain to a husband or wife that the only person they can change is themselves, thus our focus will be on what they can do to sacrificially love their partner; I'm often met with disbelief, anger, frustration, etc. Why? Because the underlying premise is that our spouse is supposed to serve US. WE are GOOD; they should see that and validate it by their actions.

What we forget as Christians is that after conversion, we still have that sinful nature and it's not inherently good. Rather, this person needs to change. I need to change. We all need to change. We need to become like Jesus—we need to crucify the self and live sacrificially. True, Jesus gives us a new identity and a new life—but we have to choose, moment-by-moment, to live that life instead of what "comes naturally (See Galatians 5: 16-26)."

What does this look like and how does it happen? Let's start by considering the metaphor Paul uses in Ephesians, Christ and His Church. Let's look at sacrifice in the Body of Christ and then apply that to our marriage relationships.

Chapter Two: The Key to Marriage—Sacrifice: Christ's & Your's

This is perhaps no better way for me to tackle this chapter than to quote from my first book, The Crucified Church. This book tackled the need for churches to "die to self so they can live for God." A large part of the book was dedicated to proving that what's good for Christians is good for Churches. I wanted church leaders to see that if we tell people to live sacrificially, we should also expect groups of Christians/Churches to do the same.

Here are a few examples from the book:

It amazes me that the same leaders who would "die on the hill" of ensuring an individual's conversion is truly based on repentance and the lordship of Christ, often fail to see that this applies to groups, i.e. churches! Do we "rightly handle the Word" by telling people to keep their old lifestyles and habits by just adding Jesus to everything "as is"? Acts 2:38 makes clear the biblical mandate to completely "turn" and go the other way. This mandate is true for individuals, why not for groups?

History bears out my premise here. Never has it been more efficient or effective to deceive into thinking renewal is good enough. Oh, it may look good at first, but eventually, the truth comes out that nothing has truly changed and the resulting conflict, hurt, and anger only make things worse. Could this be why studies show that most renewal efforts fail? Could this be why many pastors who try to slowly and patiently change their church's mission/vision "go down in flames?" I could site more stats, but every pastor I know has a friend who tried to change things only to be shot out of the sky like a clay pigeon at a skeet range! Many of you reading this are probably still "licking the wounds" of your own attempts at transformation. You don't need statistics, you need solutions!

My experience has shown me that unless people accept and commit to total surrender (self-sacrifice), they won't grow. Again, what pastor would accept the conversion and membership of a person who says, "I want salvation as a free gift—but I don't want to surrender to the lordship of Christ. I just want to add Jesus to my life as-is and get my free fire insurance for the afterlife." Such a person would no doubt be told that repentance and true faith involve 100 percent commitment and surrender—carrying our cross, thus being crucified with Christ, so that we might live (Galatians 2:20).

So why is this same standard not applied to churches? Actually, I believe it is due to several mistaken assumptions:

- *We assume that the majority of our members are saved. Based on the evident fruit (or more to the point, the lack of it) and Jesus' own prophecy regarding the lack of faith He'd find at His return, this is questionable. Jesus says "many" will be surprised to find that He "never knew" them (Matthew 7:23).*

- *We assume that just because our church members are saved, they will "default" to the Holy Spirit's guidance when it comes to the direction and focus of their local church. The fruit of history suggests that this is folly.*

- *We forget that true Christians are naturally peacemakers. Thus, when one or two "squeaky wheels" complain about a healthy, biblical mission, they can "win" since the majority will default to their position in order to maintain peace and avoid a split.*

- *We get overwhelmed by the task of trying to bring all of our members to the same point of change, like trying to get 100 clocks to chime at the same instant. It's tough! Seemingly impossible. Perhaps part of this is due to the mistaken notion that all of our people really have to agree or be at the same point. We forget that the "big mo" of momentum is what's truly necessary for change, not 100% agreement.*

- *In some cases, we assume that our Western democratic church governance is biblical. Rightly or wrongly, the majority rules and thus, what they decide is God's will. Another version of this concept is a twisted view of the "priesthood of believers" where we think that the Holy Spirit will divinely guide the majority such that it will always reflect God's will.*

How's this all working for us? Not so well.

*The truth is—just like individual believers—churches must die. They have to carry their crosses so that they may live for Christ!*2

And, from a later chapter (Chapter Three):

I tell you the truth, unless a kernel of wheat falls to the ground and dies, it remains only a single seed. But if it dies, it produces many seeds. The man who loves his life will lose it, while the man who hates his life in this world will keep it for eternal life. (John 12:24–25)

Jesus is clear here—the only way to produce fruit is to die and be regenerated with many seeds. I always think of evangelism here. I am to produce many fruit-producing seeds, not just nurture myself as one seed. But to do that, I must die. Is that not true of any church as well?

Give, and it will be given to you. A good measure, pressed down, shaken together and running over, will be poured into your lap. For with the measure you use, it will be measured to you. (Luke 6:38)

Most Christians don't believe this passage. Really! We believe that to give is to lose, not to gain. This is definitely true of many churches as well. If we give up something to reach the lost, we'll be hurt. If Luke 6:38 is true, we won't hurt and we won't lose. It says that if I try to out-give God, I'll lose (but that means I win, doesn't it?).

So when we sacrifice the organ to help a Christian rock band connect with unbelievers so they might hear the gospel and be saved, either God is a liar, or we will be blessed! If churches believed this, worship style wars and so many other sill battles would immediately cease.

Organ music is nowhere divinely ordained. And though contemporary music or instrumentation will not lead automatically to salvations, using culturally relevant musical styles removes a big hurdle for unsaved people. If they are engaged in worshiping Christ and thus drawn to Him for salvation—then let's do it! The only reason we won't is selfishness and the lack of a giving, generous spirit.

> *Therefore, if anyone is in Christ, he is a new creation; the old has gone, the new has come! (2 Corinthians 5:17)*

While I'm often critical of the conversion experiences of "believers" who have no fruit (see James 2:18), I think the biggest problem is that Christians are saved, yet ignorant of their true, new, identity in Christ. If I truly believed that I was a new creation, why on earth would I hold on to the past?

> *I have been crucified with Christ and I no longer live, but Christ lives in me. The life I live in the body, I live by faith in the Son of God, who loved me and gave himself for me. (Galatians 2:20)*

Here's the key—we live with and through Christ in us! If it's up to me, I'm toast! The good news is, I'm not living out the Christian life in my own strength. Neither is the body of Christ, the bride, Christ's church. If I remember that He gave Himself for me, what am I willing to give up for lost people I meet, or for my brothers and sisters in Christ who sit next to me in church?

And anyone who does not take his cross and follow me is not worthy of me. Whoever finds his life will lose it, and whoever loses his life for my sake will find it. (Matt 10:38–39)

One of the ugly fruits of the modern "health and wealth 'gospel'" is that it focuses on getting material gain by becoming a Christian. This false gospel promises that if one becomes a believer, he'll be rich, healthy, successful, respected, and that life will be beautiful all the time. It collapses on itself, for it cannot be reconciled with the true gospel to which persecuted Christians in places like China and Sudan cling—even at the risk of their lives. Is the true gospel worth the sacrifice of self? Are peace of mind and a clean conscience worth the sacrifice of self? Oh, yes; eternally worth it!

So why is it that churches can't even give up a denominational name that confuses or scares non-Christians? Why can't they give up ties, or robes, or the "King James only" mindset?

> *But someone may ask, "How are the dead raised? With what kind of body will they come?" How foolish! What you sow does not come to life unless it dies. When you sow, you do not plant the body that will be, but just a seed, perhaps of wheat or of something else. But God gives it a body as he has determined, and to each kind of seed he gives its own body. (1 Corinthians 15:35–38)*

When we are resurrected, this old body is not the one we get back (Can I get an amen? Glory, Hallelujah!). So why is it that when we rebirth a church, we want the old everything? Can we not trust God to give us something better?

> *What shall we say, then? Shall we go on sinning so that grace may increase? By no means! We died to sin; how can we live in it any longer? Or don't you know that all of us who were baptized into Christ Jesus were baptized into his death? We were therefore buried with him through baptism into death in order that, just as Christ was raised from the dead through the glory of the Father, we too may live a new life. (Romans 6:1–4)*

When we grasp the power of this passage, our lives and the collective life of the church will change forever! We truly are dead to sin. It's gone. We now have the power to reject and walk away from it. We don't have to walk in drunkenness, sexual sin, selfish ignorance of our unchurched neighbors. We don't need to come to virtual blows in our church business meetings anymore—that is dead. Or at least it can be. We can really live a new life!

Every pastor, elder, deacon, or ministry leader worth his or her salt would passionately agree that without a total surrender and dedication to the truth of Romans 6:1-4, a person cannot be saved, let alone live a godly, sanctified life! While we may interpret the verses differently, the bottom line is the same—personal salvation and total surrender to the lordship of Christ are inextricably connected, if not synonymous.

But what about churches?

While I'll save my ecclesiology for a later chapter, I would suggest that every evangelical leader knows that the church is a collective group, set apart or called out by God. In other words, what in principle applies to individuals will inevitably be carried over to churches since the church is the sum total of those individuals.

The church is people. It's not a building, corporation, denomination, or set of programs. The church is a group of saved, called-out believers, established in the truths taught by Christ and the apostles, inclusive of the five primary purposes of God, Worship, Evangelism, Ministry, Discipleship, and Fellowship), and entrusted to elders who meet the criteria of 1 Timothy 3 and Titus 1. 2 3

Finally,

So most of what applies to individuals, applies to the collective body of Christ:

- *She must carry her cross daily, remembering that she is dead to self, but alive in Christ.*
- *She must know that she exists only through and for Christ.*
- *She must constantly die to the old and give birth to the new.*

- *She must give and thus be blessed.*
- *She must continually lose her life to find true life.*
- *She must participate in the death, burial, and resurrection of Jesus—thus receiving a new church life, not just a warmed-over, old congregation.*
- *She must have and embrace a new identity in Christ.*

What does this look like?

In many ways, it's invisible. It's an internal commitment to do and become anything in order to obey and follow Jesus. Most commonly, it springs into action and thus becomes visible when a challenge is presented. That challenge could be to reach a new people group taking root in the community. For example, in retrospect, I'm convinced that the decline of many modern churches actually started in the 1960s when so many Caucasians fled the inner city and its ethnic changes to take refuge in the suburbs.

WWJD (What Would Jesus Do)? Jesus would have stayed and reached out to African American families, Hispanic families, and families of all other races, as they came into the neighborhood. The church would have reflected the diversity of the community around her. Instead, she withdrew to a "safe" place based on her own comfort and desire.

The internal commitment to change would result in external action to do whatever is necessary to reach a lost, confused, and dying younger generation with the gospel. While this change should never involve surrendering the message of the gospel, it almost always means sacrificing some methods we use to share it. 4

What About Couples?

Could it be that since individual Christians are called to "die to self," and churches are called to "die to self," that couples should too? Absolutely, yes! Could some of the sacrifices made by church members to create unity with others or help open the door for new people be the same or at least similar to sacrifices people must make for their spouses in marriage? Oh yeah! Yes, yes YES!

You KNEW I was going to "go there" didn't you?

The bad news is that it's hard to live a crucified life. The good news is that Jesus does it in us and the results are fantastic! Speaking of the church, we know that this works based on the example of Christ and the Church. Jesus laid down his life for the church and when she responds the same way, POWERFUL things happen. Paul even surprises his readers in Ephesians chapter 5 by telling them that all his instructions about marriage in that letter were REALLY about Christ and the Church (Eph. 5:32).

Couples are actually called to live-out their marriage so as to demonstrate God's nature and the relationship between Christ and the Church. Thus, marriage is NOT about his happiness or her happiness primarily, but about the gospel being proclaimed through their relationship. This can only happen through sacrifice.

Think about this. In the beginning, God said, "Let us make man in our image (Gen. 1:26)." Then, scripture tells us that to accomplish this, "God made man in His image, male and female (Gen. 1:27)." Later, in chapter two of Genesis, we read, "Therefore, a man shall leave his mother and cling to his wife and they shall become one (Gen.2:24)." So man and woman, joined in marriage as one, reflect the image of God more completely than either of them could alone!

That's powerful—and intimidating as well! We have an awesome responsibility and exciting opportunity here!

This also explains why scripture is so replete with instructions about submitting, loving, and respecting, "as unto the Lord," (Eph. 5:22 et al). I lay down my life for my wife as if she were Jesus who already laid down His life for me. If she's nasty and in a rotten mood, I still sacrifice for her because ultimately (sorry honey), it's REALLY for Jesus! I'm reflecting His nature and Character by loving her when she's not loving me back—or at least not acting like she does!

This is truly an act of faith. If I didn't know and trust Jesus to help me and to honor my commitment to loving, I couldn't do it when my wife isn't doing it back. If I live the "get way" and think marriage is a "tit for tat" kind of partnership where I'm in it as long as my needs are met, then I could only serve Karen my wife if she's serving me. On the other hand, if I believe that Jesus will care for and bless me for giving when there's nothing humanly/physically coming back to me, I can truly give and live a crucified life!

Crucified Marriages: Unique, Distinct, yet One

Jesus taught that the oneness in marriage was more than just a physical connection. Rather than just stating that, as Moses taught, husband and wife become "one flesh;" they are "no longer two, but one (Matt. 19:6)." This means that marriage creates a unity that is emotional, physical, spiritual, etc., while remaining distinctly man and woman, there's a third reality here where the couple is now in a supernatural way—ONE new creation.

We see this with Christ and his church, a point Paul expounds in Ephesians 5 as well. The church is his body. She is one with Him. We call her "the body of Christ" and rightly so. Yet, we still know that Jesus is distinctly the Son of God, the second person of the Trinity, thus not the same "person" as the Father or the Holy Spirit. We also recognize the distinction between Jesus and the collective Church with all her flaws and foibles. Still, it IS interesting that Jesus' sacrifice and his grace-filled view of the Church is that she is perfect and flawless.

There is so much here, but for now, suffice it to say that seeing marriage as a new, unified entity—not just as a partnership between two innately selfish people—puts us on a path to success, just as our understanding of the oneness of the Trinity or the oneness of Christ with his Church Bride gives us Theological and Ecclesiological possibilities as well. The point is, since we're one, we seek to point to the perfect, triune nature of God by serving our spouse FOR God. This is a FAR cry from seeking to find fulfillment or pleasure from our spouse!

<u>Valuing and Sacrificing for the Differences</u>

Gary Smalley in his video series, "Hidden Keys to Lasting Relationships," tells the story of a man and woman fighting in front of him during a counseling session.5 After listening for several minutes, Gary interrupted the couple to ask, "Do you have children?" "Why yes," they answered. So, without batting an eye,

Gary asked, "How did THAT happen?" "Well, you know…the normal way," was the husband's awkward response. "No," Gary corrected him, "I'll tell you how it happened…you valued the differences."

I love this story because of its ramifications far beyond sex and marriage. While they are one in marriage, men and women are different (contrary to what is portrayed in popular movies and culture). As such, they have different needs. Thus, sacrifice on each other's behalf takes on a different meaning/application as well.

As explained in the popular book and video series, "Love and Respect," Paul's admonition in Ephesians 5:33 shows us that the primary needs of men and women differ.6 Men need to feel respect as a primary measure of relationship satisfaction. Women, on the other hand, need to feel loved and cherished. With this in mind, the sacrifice each offers to the other will, if successful, contribute to meeting these basic, yet primary needs.

But this isn't "natural." In other words, since men value respect, they are more likely to naturally give respect in ways they'd like to receive it—thinking this will satisfy their spouse. Conversely, women value love and a nurturing cherished approach which naturally flows from them toward their husbands. They thus miss each other. In addition, since men value respect, they are less likely to respond lovingly when they feel dis-respected. Women will rarely show respect when they feel unloved. Complicating things further, women and men respect different things. So it's hard for a wife to show respect for her husband when he does things she doesn't find respectable.

And so goes the negative cycle…

Then, as if things weren't difficult already, we add the challenge of differing love languages. As per the popular book, individuals (male or female) have different ways they receive love—aka. love languages. For some it's acts of kindness, others need words of affirmation/affection, still others prefer physical touch. Therefore, even IF I understand that my wife's primary need is to feel loved and I sacrifice my selfish focus on wanting respect to give her that love, I may mess-up if I don't know and use her personal love language!

Seven years into our marriage, we almost gave-up. I remember coming into the kitchen, tossing a spoon onto the counter, and heading out the door to an appointment. I was a newly ordained and hired full-time pastor with "darkness to dispel." I was literally, "on a mission from God." (Yes, the Blues Brothers would have been proud.)

As I raced out the door, my beautiful wife said, "I won't be here when you get back." "Oh?" I replied clue-less-ly, "are you going shopping?" "No," she responded calmly, "I'm going to Canada." I quickly realized that she wasn't talking about a surprise visit to her parents in Ontario, but rather a move with the kids to escape feeling unloved and neglected.

Ouch!

After hours of conversation and many tears, I realized that by neglecting my wife's primary need and her love language of acts of service, I had been telling her for 7 years that I loved everyone else, but not her.7 She felt broken, hurt, and used-up. I had nearly crushed her spirit…but by God's grace and with her patience, I was able to catch it in time and reverse the pattern.

It took time and patience to change things. I had to redo my approach to our marriage completely. I remember that at first, she didn't trust that things were really changing and even "pushed my buttons" a few times by spurning my new-found-approach to showing her love. Still, I'll never forget the day—I can close my eyes and see it in vivid Technicolor—when she came-up behind me, grabbed my arms, and when I spun around she smiled and with a tear in her eye said, "You really DO love me...don't you!"

Twenty-three awesome years later I can tell you, this marriage thing is tough! Tough, but so worth it!

Throughout my ministry, I've always maintained that God created marriage as the perfect crucible for character building change. I love me. Thus, being alone with me is easy. Furthermore, if I had spent the last 30 years with myself and no other intimate, committed relationships, I KNOW I'd still have many of the rough edges and flaws I had 30 years ago. Marriage forces those things to be dealt with as does no other institution or experience. It's not easy—not for the "feint at heart." Still, it's worth it!! Today, we love being together and have loads of fun serving, working, or just watching movies. There is nobody I'd rather spend time with and vise-versa.

In many ways, I believe God created marriage as the perfect character-building crucible. Think about it—he created two people who are polar opposites, made them insatiably attracted to each other, and watched the proverbial "sparks fly" as they came together. The bad news is that they'd inevitably fight when they got together yet they can't help but be drawn to one another nonetheless. The good news is that if they survive these atomic encounters and the chaos of their disagreements, BOTH of them will come away stronger and more like their Creator than they were before. The key is to know this and commit to working out the rough edges until that unity and God-reflection can occur.

Part of the foundation of this process is the recognition of what we often call "the male ego" and the "woman's intuition." In our unisex, genderless society, it's not politically correct to talk about these things. Still, if we're going to make marriage work, we must address the reality of the male/female distinctions or we're destined to trip over them daily.

For example, I believe that "women's intuition" has to do with relationships. I believe that most women instinctively know that certain things are "good" and/or "bad" in a typical relationship. Men don't have this innate, God-given relational common sense. On the other hand, I believe that men have an ego which generates assertiveness, protectiveness, and drive. There are exceptions to these generalities I admit, still, the trends are obvious to even the most casual observer.

The problem comes when the woman THINKS that her mate has the same relational "common sense" that she has. Thus, if he does something that could be considered rude or inconsiderate, she ASSUMES he did it on purpose since it seemed too obvious to have been unintended/accidental. When she complains, the husband feels disrespected and maybe even harassed or "henpecked" such that he lashes out or retreats to his "man cave" and ignores her. This cycle normally ends poorly—to say the least!

In order to fix this, two things must happen:

1. The wife must exercise patience and not assume that her husband "knows" how his behavior hurt her. She must be willing to kindly guide him to see and understand her feelings.
2. The husband must "swallow his pride" and ask for help with these relationship issues. He must also exercise patience and become a bit "thick skinned" when his wife becomes impatient with things she believes are "common sense" regarding their marriage.

To that end, there are a few techniques and habits which, if learned early on, can make marriage fun, productive, and much easier. My goal in this book is to share those with you—some learned by person trial and a lot of error, others learned by helping hundreds of others through the same challenges. The first, and perhaps most important of these techniques is—effective or, more accurately, sacrificial communication.

Chapter Three: Sacrificial Communication.

The key to good communication is understanding, but understanding necessitates sacrifice. In his best-selling book, Seven Habits of Highly Effective People, author Stephen Covey promoted the idea that we should "Seek First To Understand, Then to be Understood."8 In scripture, James said it this way, "let every person be quick to hear, slow to speak, slow to anger (1:19, ESV)."

Being quick to hear or seeking first to hear requires a great deal of self-control and self-sacrifice, especially when arguing. If I'm in an argument, I want to win. If I want to win, I'm always trying to formulate a statement or response that will silence my opponent before she comes up with one to silence me! I'm not really listening to understand what's in her heart, I'm listening to formulate a killer argument. That's the human, selfish norm.

When my wife and I do couples counseling, we use two tools popularized by Life Innovations, Inc. and their Prepare-Enrich program.9 The first tool is assertiveness using what I call, "I-language." I'll come back to this. The second tool is the use of reflective listening. Of the two, this is the hardest to learn and yet is the more powerful communication device I've ever witnessed.

When reflectively listening, a person repeats back what they've heard their partner say, using their own words, until their partner says, "That's it! You've understood me." Then—and ONLY then—the listener is allowed to express his/her own view and the roles reverse. The goal for the listener is not to necessarily agree, but to clearly and completely understand what their partner is saying. In fact, they may totally disagree with what's being said, but can still demonstrate that they've heard. Sometimes, they get to "hear" what their partner is NOT saying. Sometimes, they don't just understand their partner…they help their partner understand themselves!

Larry and Kellie

A few years ago, I was doing premarital counseling with a beautiful young couple. I'll call them Larry and Kellie. Larry was a pastor's son—young, handsome, smart, and likeable. Kellie was a beautiful musician, newly graduated from college and working for a small church as a choir director and keyboard player. When I asked them to practice the use of "I language" and "Reflective Listening," a miraculous thing happened…and I got to witness it.

Before I describe the scene in more detail, let me quickly define "I language." "I language" is an assertiveness tool where the speaker uses the word "I" more than "you." So for example, if I want my wife to pick up her mail left lying around the house, I might normally say, "You need to pick us your mess. You always leave junk lying around. You're driving me crazy!" That would likely result in an argument or the silent treatment (fight or flight) as a response. As an alternative, I can use "I language" by saying,

"Honey, I have a problem. I get very agitated and I feel stressed when there's a lot of clutter. I would feel more at peace if you could try to keep your mail in one place or toss it if you don't want it. I want to be less stressed toward you. I don't want the clutter to be a conflict because I love you."

With "I language," I'm saying the same thing, but "owning" the issue and framing it in a way that's less threatening to my spouse.

OK, now back to Larry and Kellie. As an exercise, I asked them individually to write down three things they'd like more or less of in their relationship and how they'd each feel if these things came to pass. I told them not to share them with their partner yet, just to write them down so we could share them using "I language" and "Reflective Listening."

When it came time to share, Kellie went first. She looked into Larry's eyes and said, "I wish we could be more spontaneous."

Larry looked at me. I quickly directed him to look at her and reflect. He said, "So…you want us to be more 'off the cuff…right?" "Yeah…" she said hesitantly. Then they both stared at me as if they'd just pretended to listen to a four hour lecture in ancient Gaelic.

I looked at Kellie and said, "That's not all you're looking for—is it?" "No" she replied. So I looked at Larry and told him to ask her a question. "Can you give me an example?" "Sure," she said. "Remember that time we were driving and saw that carnival on the side of the road. We stopped and ended up spending the day. We had cotton candy and rode rides. We laughed and laughed. It was awesome!" "So," Larry stuttered, "You want us to do things that aren't planned…right?" "Yeah…" she said sheepishly.

It was at that moment that I realized something important. The beautiful thing is, Larry recognized it also. Kellie didn't know how to express what she wanted. She wasn't even clear on it herself—

she just instinctively knew that something was missing. Instantly, Larry was "all over it." "OK, OK," he started, "So tell me this—besides the fact that it wasn't planned, what WAS it about that day that made it so special?" "Oh…that's a great question," Kellie said, "I think it was that we didn't talk on our phones, we didn't have to rush, we never looked at our watches, our conversations weren't interrupted…." "Wait!" Larry exclaimed, "I think I've got it! What made that day so perfect was that it was focused time. I focused on you. You focused on me. We weren't distracted by all the projects and people and schedules we're always slaves to. What I think you want is more focused time for our relationship. That's what I want too. I love you!"

Kelly stood up and with tears in her eyes; she hugged Larry like he had just returned from a tour of duty in Iraq. I felt like it was a holy moment and I should sneak out of the room to leave the two of them alone. It was beautiful! Why? Because, not only had Larry used reflective listening to hear his sweetheart's words, he had heard her heart. Not only did he hear what she said, he heard what she didn't say. Not only did he make sure he understood her—he helped her understand herself! And that my friends, is miraculous.

Now let's suppose Larry thought Kellie's desire or idea here was ridiculous. Let's say he felt that they had plenty of time alone and plenty of focused relationship time away from family and friends and schedules, etc. Let's say Larry was frankly sick and tired of spending one-on-one time and really missed spending time with all of their friends. Let's say, Larry felt pressed to share this with Kellie because his social butterfly need was dying on the proverbial branch!

The fact that he had heard Kellie and helped her understand her own need would go a long way in helping her be open to him sharing an opposing view, would it not? Further, if Larry was willing to sacrifice some of this to help Kellie feel more loved, do you suppose Kellie's desire would be do sacrifice as well? What would be the likelihood of Kellie compromising by giving a few more hours of social crowd time if Larry had understood her heart, validated it, and FIRST given her more alone time by his own free will choice?

But that's not how we think is it? We're taught to "take care of number one." We're told that we must fight for our personal rights. We're encouraged to "stand up for ourselves." We're told that the key is to take care of our needs so we will (supposedly) be better willing and able to take care of others. In the scenario above, some might question whether or not Kellie and Larry should even be together since they have such different ideas of social interaction. Maybe the solution would be for Kellie to find another introvert and Larry to find another extrovert so that their needs could be met. Isn't that the goal after all? To get all we can get from our partner?

No. It isn't the goal. Not based on the teaching and example of the one who created marriage. God does NOT see marriage as the ultimate need-satisfying-machine that we presume it to be. Don't misunderstand, marriage can and often does satisfy. Ironically however, it is more likely to do this when we give, not when we seek to take. When I "seek first to understand" my wife, I'm more likely to be understood BY my wife. As Jesus promised, when I give to Karen, it is "given to (me), full measure, pressed down, shaken together…overflowing…. (Luke 6:38)."

What God Hears

Another element of communication has nothing to do with my listening skills or my spouses'. No, it has to do with what God hears. And yes, that would be every-thing! We'll touch on this in a later chapter, but even if my spouse has bananas in both ears, God hears all. If my communication is righteous, I can trust that God hears and will bless—even if my spouse does not. That's comforting, but it's also motivating. God is my source of satisfaction. As such, my communication with Karen is more about my love for Him than it is with her ability to hear and respond to me. True sacrificial, crucified communication is based on this fact. Nothing else will work.

To trust God to take care of me and to fill my needs even if my spouse doesn't, I must come to know His true nature. I MUST believe he loves me more than I could ever love myself. I must believe He knows all and wants to bless me, not harm me. I must believe the biblical revelation of an all-powerful, yet all-loving and merciful God. If I do believe in Him, then I know he'll take care of me when I sacrifice for my spouse—even if she fails to respond.

Having said this, it is my experience that 80% of marriage problems can be solved by true reflective listening and the use of "I language." The other 20% are dealt with using solid, habitual, consistent conflict resolution techniques. We'll deal with that in the next chapter.

Chapter Four: Sacrificial Conflict Resolution

So, here's the typical scenario. He says "X." She says, "Y." He makes a detailed analytical case for "X." She still says, "Y," but says it louder. He attacks "Y" with facts, spreadsheets, and a passionate appeal. She says "X" is "Stupid" and starts to cry. He says something he'll regret later, as does she, before they both exit the room rapidly, slamming doors and uttering expletives.

Sound familiar?

I've known couples who have repeated this form of communication for years, all the time wondering why they can't get along and perhaps concluding that they are just "different people" and will never reconcile their differences. So sad…and completely untrue.

I once had a couple in my office argue about an issue for 45 minutes. Why did I let it go that long? Because they agreed! At first, I thought I was missing something. After 25 minutes or so, I realized that I wasn't missing anything, but they were. I let it go longer because I thought at any minute they'd realize they were in agreement on the core issues and stop fighting. Instead, they just got louder and louder and more upset.

Finally, I yelled "STOP!!" I looked at her and said, "Do you believe X, Y, and Z?" She said she did. I then told her to be quiet and turned to him. "Do YOU believe X, Y, and Z?" He said "Yes." "OK then," I concluded, "you just argued for 45 minutes over something you agree on. In what parallel universe does that make sense, because it doesn't make ANY sense in this one does it?!"

Admittedly, I was a bit strong with them, but I'd had enough. Now their problem was a lack of listening and good communication as per the last chapter. Still, what I've also learned over the years is that couples often continue these bad habits because they lack a good conflict resolution strategy. Somehow, they reason that if they just keep arguing and restating their case, something will magically or, supernaturally change. God has given us tools for resolving conflict. If we choose not to use them, He's under no obligation to stop us from fighting. After all, remember the definition of insanity: doing the same thing over and over, while expecting different results.

Over the years, my wife and I have had great results using Life Innovations, "10 Steps to Resolving Couple Conflict."10 This tool, part of the Prepare-Enrich program, (see www.prepare-enrich.com), is a real blessing. Let me list the steps and then share some comments about using the steps:

1. Choose a time and place for discussion.
2. Define the problem, be specific.
3. List how each person/group contributes to the problem.

4. List past attempts to resolve the issue that were not successful.
5. Brainstorm; list at least 10 possible solutions.
6. Discuss and evaluate each of these possible solutions.
7. Agree on one solution to try.
8. Agree on how you will each work toward this solution. Be specific.
9. Set-up another meeting to discuss your progress.
10. Reward each other for progress.

These steps and this process are nothing short of brilliant! First of all, notice how the first few steps guide you to be psychologically in agreement before the disagreement/conflict is even being addressed. You agree on when and where to discuss it, you agree on what the problem is, etc. Also, notice how critical, yet succinct each step is. For example, step one. I have witnessed couples who fight just because one is a morning person and the other is not. In addition, one might be a "Type A Personality" such that they want things fixed, "NOW," while their partner needs time to process and think about things. If they agree on a time and place, the "Type A" is satisfied that while things may not get resolved immediately, they won't be "swept under the rug." At the same time, their partner has time to think and plan prior to the discussion.

These steps, while hard to practice habitually since they involve dramatic habit changes, are powerful and extremely effective when couples put them to use consistently. Still, let me give you some "bullet point" advice to keep in mind when using these and how they are sacrificial:

- Step two de-personalizes the problem. This step allows the couple to make the problem into a "thing we're fixing together, "instead of something one or the other is responsible for alone. Frankly, when we understand the unity of marriage as Jesus taught it, "no longer two, but one

(Matt. 19:6), it is ridiculous to lay blame on one person in the marriage anyway. In fact, it's impossible!

- Steps 3 and 8 involve self-disclosure and self-commitment. In other words, if my wife and I are doing them, this is NOT the time for me to tell her how she contributes or what she should do about it. No, this is MY time to "come clean" and make a commitment to change. It's self-sacrificial in admission and promise to perform.

- Step four avoids insanity. You know the definition of insanity which states that doing the same things over and over while expecting different results! We are creatures of habit and unless we eliminate the repetition of failed solutions, we're likely to repeat them.

- Brainstorming involves the sacrificial act of "zip-it." What I mean is that when you do brainstorming, you have to allow both you and your partner to have a judgment-free period of creative expression. The moment one of you says, "Ha ha, that's the most ridiculous idea I've ever heard," you're brainstorming session will end because the creativity will cease. I once was involved in a corporate brainstorming session where someone suggested that the best way to reach people at a highly-secure government research center was for someone to don a gorilla costume and hand out bananas with letters attached at the gate. Dumb? Well since he would have likely been arrested or shot, yes! But knowing the rules of brainstorming, we dutifully wrote "Gorilla Suit" on the flipchart and kept going. Couples need to do the same. We recommend listing at least 10 ideas in brainstorming before moving on to the next step.

- The goal of step six isn't to shoot down each other's ideas like clay pigeons at a skeet shooting range. Rather, you only eliminate the really bad ones, (like the gorilla suit).

It's GREAT to have several good ones left after step six. Calmly taking your partner's comments about why your idea might be less-than-ideal is another example of marital sacrifice.

- Steps 9 and 10 are critical, but many couples skip them. It got so bad early in my ministry to couples, that I started telling them that I would refuse to see them again unless they finished these first. There were a few who never returned. This is so sad because I have learned that without 9 and 10, the entire process is a waste of time and may even make matters worse. Why? Because we often return to old patterns after trying something new for a while. When we go back to old patterns, we assume that the new idea(s) failed and thus our marriage is "hopeless." Better to have never tried and be upset than to have tried, slid backwards, and assumed that we are doomed! Now, I teach couples to set a date for step nine IMMEDIATELY after agreeing on a solution to try. This is important so that they can redirect to another idea from their brainstorming if their solution fails (usually a couple of weeks is necessary to make sure it really isn't working). It's also important to meet again so they can reinforce and encourage each other if the solution they choose IS working!

- And that brings us to step 10. I always point out that the wording of step 10 is critical. They reward each other for PROGRESS, not perfection. First, the reward must be based on your partner's love language so that it's meaningful to him/her. Second, progress is the key. The example I always use is that if my agreement to work on our household messiness problem was that I would remove my shoes from the living room floor each evening, and for two weeks, I've removed one shoe; my wife has a chose to make in our follow-up meeting. She COULD say, "Hey bonehead—how many feet did God give you. Let's count them. That would be TWO! So how many shoes go with the two feet? That's right—T-W-O! So why have you been leaving one on the floor you dope!?" If she DID respond this way, my inclination would be to take my tools and make the other show a permanent part of the floor using half-dozen wood screws! On the other hand, if she said, (after counting to 10 and praying for help), "Honey, I've noticed that you've been putting away one of your shoes…thank you. That's progress," I'd probably wait for her to leave the room, run to put away the other shoe, and then stand there sheepishly waiting for her to notice so I'd get an "ata-boy."

Before we close this chapter, let me address what I call "Conflict Zombies." Like the zombies in popular TV shows and movies, "Conflict Zombies" are dead, but they don't seem to know they're dead, so they keep coming back.

They chase you around and hound you till you give in to them—or kill them, again, for the last time.

How?

First, we have to recognize that we've already killed them. If we used the 10 Steps successfully, we should go back to what worked instead of letting the old patterns rule us! Second, if the solution we originally tried has ceased to work, go back to the brainstorming list and try another one. Whatever you do, don't let the zombies win—they're DEAD! This resurrection of the dead problems happens in many areas. Still the most common…I'm sure you can guess…is regarding money!

Chapter Five: Dying to Your Budget

One of the best decisions my wife and I made after getting engaged was to combine checking accounts and shift our thinking from "your money or my money," to "our money!" True, it was a challenge since we weren't living together, but even the habit of setting up dates to do budget planning, pay bills, or balance the checkbook was a good thing for us to establish early on.

Far too often, I see couples who've been married for years and yet still have a "yours" or "mine" attitude when it comes to money. It's ironic that even when husbands and wives think this way, the IRS doesn't, nor does the judicial system in the case of bad debt, bankruptcy, etc. You can separate accounts and funds all you like, but if one of you dies, creditors will come after joint assets—all of them if necessary. Thus, it makes no sense to pretend these things are separate when you really aren't and nobody else will "play along" if you continue this ruse.

Any supposed benefits to separating funds are far outweighed by the advantages of having a unified financial plan and process. Having said all this, I'm not opposed to budgeting a certain amount of money for him to spend for fun or for her to spend as discretionary. The difference is that even that amount is agreed on by both partners working literally from the "same (budget) page."

Since most couples consist of one saver and one spender, here's where sacrifice comes in. The saver must "die to self" by giving some "blow money" to the spender every pay period. Conversely, the spender must crucify his/her flesh by reigning in enough spending to save. Normally, when this happens, the net result is great—a very balanced financial plan. Without sacrifice, chaos rules!

What we're talking about here is dying to self-management, self-sufficiency, and self-direction in lieu of a biblical synergy or oneness despite your two-ness. You chose to marry. Thus God united you. Now, you must lay down your life as your spouse should to make this new entity healthy and successful.

Two important parts of this are budgeting and goal-setting. I recommend starting with goals. A popular book in the 80's was <u>If You Don't Know Where You're Going; You'll Probably End-up Somewhere Else</u> by Dr. David P. Campbell.11 Practically, how can you budget effectively if you don't know what you're trying to accomplish together. Furthermore, if you have different goals and therefore, a different agenda, budgeting won't work because one or both of you will break the budget plan regularly.

I suggest the following:
1. Plan a date to set 5, 10, and 20 year goals together.
2. Between now and then, each of you write-out your own version of these.

3. Talk them through and agree on a written set of goals for each time period. You can "flesh-this-out" by setting health, family, financial, spiritual, and other goal categories.
4. Once you've agreed on the goals. Each of you should fill-out a budget sheet (we've provided one for you in the Appendix of this book).
5. Then, meet again to compare budgets and agree on a final version you'll both support.

To that end, let me share a few more thoughts on budgeting. First, do yourselves a favor and read Dave Ramsey's Total Money Makeover and enroll in his "Financial Peace University" course at a local church.12 It will change your life regarding debt—one of the primary sources of pain in marriage. Second, I'd strongly recommend reading Bank On Yourself by Pamela Yellen.13 Yellen reveals some little-known methods of safely saving while leveraging your investments to survive day-to-day.

I'd also suggest that you consider sitting with a counselor to do the Prepare-Enrich program we mentioned earlier. Budgeting is just one piece of what they do, but a helpful one nonetheless.

Chapter Six: Sacrificial Sex?

Second only to money, sex is a leading cause of marital stress, separation, and divorce. Whether it's a difference in sexual desire or an affair, sexual issues can tear apart a relationship. On the other hand, as God intended it, sex can be the glue that helps keep couples together. The key to having sex be a positive force in marriage is, you guessed it…sacrifice.

Before we explore this further, we should consider what I call, "The façade of sex as a basic need." In the U.S. and throughout most of Western Europe, we've been conditioned to believe that all people need to have sex and that without it; we are psychologically and perhaps even spiritually deficient or ill. Movies like "The 40 Year Old Virgin" teach young people that anyone who doesn't have sex is odd, or sick.

This idea affects marriage in that we come to believe that if we're not having sex as often as we like—or at least as often as one partner likes—we MUST be divorced or at least be allowed to cheat or use pornography since, sex is a primary need. If a partner gets sick or just loses interest due to age, menopause, or a mid-life crisis, we panic—or worse.

As an aside, this is also why the idea of sexual compatibility is also a farce. Couples who live together are more likely to become divorced than couple who don't live together before marriage. The idea that you must "try before you buy" sexually is ridiculous based the studies that have been done on premarital sexual experience and its impact on marital success. But even if it was true that sexual experience before marriage helped ensure sexual compatibility, the reality of change due to health, age, stress, and other factors negates that benefit.

In other words, if you're 100% sexually compatible and enjoy the same interests in frequency and positions for intercourse, etc., today; it's entirely probable that this will change over time. My question to you is—then what? Will you quit? If your marriage and frankly your sex life is only built on your own pleasure, the answer to that question is, sadly, "Yes."

So, when God tells us to save sex for a monogamous marriage between one man and one woman, He really does know what he's talking about! It actually works—when we understand that sex is the icing on the marital cake, not the cake itself. It isn't a basic need without which we die or become mentally warped. On the other hand it's a beautiful uniting factor for couples who use it correctly and sacrificially.

Psychologically, and physiologically, sex is more satisfying when the focus is giving to the other person. This is ironic when we consider that the focus of sex in our culture is personal satisfaction or pleasure. This is not to say that we can be 100% happy simply by satisfying our partner. The key is focus—the priority is giving to our spouse with a desire to also achieve sexual satisfaction.

The key to making this work is communication. I've noticed over the years that, apart from medical issues such as Erectile Dysfunction, (which is more than treatable in most cases), the majority of sexual problems in marriage can be resolved by improving communication. When couples learn how to share their sexual likes and dislikes then it's possible to give and improve intimacy. This communication is both verbal and non-verbal. And, like all communication, it involves both sending and receiving information. Reflecting what you've "heard" or "understood" from your spouse by repeating what was said or by acting on it in bed is the key to completing this sexual communication loop.

It's also important to consider creativity and the role it plays in romance. Sometimes romance and routine are contradictory. Not only do most couples find that changing things up a bit sexually helps, it's also part of communication in that without trying new things, it's hard to know what each partner likes or doesn't like. The point is, don't get stuck in a rut, use variety to find out what your loved one enjoys and then provide that. You will likely be surprised at how much that pleases your spouse. You'll be even MORE surprised at how much this pleases you!

The Apostle Paul wrote, "*The husband should fulfill his marital duty to his wife, and likewise the wife to her husband. The wife does not have authority over her own body but yields it to her husband. In the same way, the husband does not have authority over his own body but yields it to his wife. Do not deprive each other except perhaps by mutual consent and for a time, so you may devote yourselves to prayer. Then come together again so that Satan will not tempt you because of your lack of self-control* (I Cor. 7:3-5)."

What we have here is a beautiful sacrificial balance. When our attention is on the needs of our partner, both in terms of frequency of sexual intimacy as well as the type/approach to giving them pleasure, a bond is created and a protection exists against the temptations of a fallen world. In this context, romantic times and positive sexual experiences also create positive memories. Why is that important? We'll explore this in depth in chapter seven.

Chapter Seven: Crucified Fun Times?

When counseling couples, I'm amazed at how often they list leisure activities as least important or irrelevant to their marital success. This is true of both engaged couples and couples who've been married for years. "Having fun?" they often ask, "How can THAT help solve our problems?"

For this reason, it's common to see these couples spending very little if any time together other than in the mundane activities of life. Further, if they DO have fun times, husband and wife are often involved separately. In other words, he bowls and she goes skating or he hunts while she skis, etc. While having individual "his" and "hers" hobbies is a good idea, it's NOT good to have zero, "OUR" activities just for fun.

Why?

Human beings tend to focus on the negative. If you doubt this, just look at the titles on the newspapers and magazines at your local supermarket checkout line. Bad news sells. Dirty laundry sells. And for couples, the focus on problems and challenges will typically far outweigh their focus on their strengths in their relationship. The problem is that as these problems grow or swell, the negatively becomes overwhelming! Soon, everything—even the good things—is viewed through a dark, discouraging lens.

This negative foundation leads to a negative downward spiral. Every time a couple sits down to resolve a conflict, it's shrouded by darkness, discouragement, and hopelessness. Leisure activities—fun times together can break this cycle and create a positive backdrop for healthy conflict resolution and productive communication.

For example, how much better would a discussion about finances go if you went hiking, had a nice dinner out, and then sat in a café having mocha latte's while you discussed savings? Hmmm? Sounds MUCH better than slugging it out at 6 AM before running off to work...late...in a funk!

Here's what I suggest. If you don't have much fun time together or perhaps you haven't found hobbies you both enjoy doing together, try making a list of 10 things you'd each like to try. Then, sit down over a warm beverage and discuss them. Pick one or two you'd both be willing to try together and see if you can create a new, fun activity to participate in as a couple. You may be surprised at how this affects your relationship!

Now I would be disloyal to the theme of this book if I didn't point-out that choosing hobbies or fun activities involves sacrifice. There's more than a slight chance that when you sit-down to discuss your ideas of hobbies/activities to try, you will have two very different lists. If one of you loves the outdoors and the other's idea of camping is the Hilton Hotel, you're going to face a challenge. This will ONLY work if you each sacrifice to find common ground and pleasure. For instance, the outdoorsman might have to try roller-skating and the homebody might have to go for a hike or two—but is it worth it? Will God bless it? Will you be more than thankful that you at least tried it? YES—YES—YES!!!

Another important element of this is vacation time. I'm amazed at how many American couples never take a vacation together. We're either too busy, too broke, or too disinterested to bother. Yet, many of us find that our fondest childhood memories are of family vacations. These become experiential legacies—events and stories passed on for generations to come.

Ironically, some of the fondest and funniest memories come from what I call, "vacations gone awry." People love to talk about, "The time our tent collapsed at 3 AM in a snowstorm on the rim of the Grand Canyon," or, "The time we were chased by a bear in

Canada," or, "The time the car broke down in the middle of the desert." So, even the worst vacation becomes a more positive and happy memory than the best day at work. There's a lesson in that somewhere....

One of our favorites is the time we took our entire church youth group camping in Western NY. Mid-way through our stay, the campground was hit by a violent rain and thunderstorm. Actually, a tornado touched-down nearby, but we didn't see or hear about it till later. Karen and I gathered-up all the kids and raced them to the concrete bath house near our campsite. As we all huddled in the doorway watching the sheets of rain and wind—rain often coming horizontally across our field of vision, I noticed a river washing through the middle of the campground. It was a small flash-flood and it ran right through the middle of several tents. "Look," I shouted, "That poor guy has a river in his tent!" Everyone laughed until one of the teens screamed, "Look Joel—I think that's YOUR tent!" She was right. And we spent the next 12 hours in the local

Laundromat drying clothes, sleeping bags, etc. Still, some 25 years later, we love to talk about "that time the tornado hit our campground."

Vacations, (good or bad), are important, but then need not be expensive. Again, some of our favorites were very affordable. Camping is a favorite for our family. When the kids were little, it was in tents. I remember tossing gear in the back of our Dodge Aries complete with 90 pound lab, two "rug rats," Momma and I for a week's adventure in the Shenandoah Valley. Gas and camp fees were the only added cost since food was what we would have eaten anyway and our activities (swimming, hiking, playing hide-and-seek, etc.) were all provided by God.

Whatever your pleasure—take time away and take it away as a couple. Spend time having fun and do this all the more when you're struggling in your relationship. It's worth it! And, speaking of being alone…let's talk about another sensitive issue, letting go of family and friends to focus on each other….

Chapter Eight: Family & Friends—Letting Go...

As we explore the subject of extended family, I'm reminded of a story. The mayor of a small town was under constant criticism by the local residents. Having grown-up in that town, everyone knew him and his family, but that didn't stop the constant grumbling over his policies, appointments, speeches, and more.

One day a visitor from out of State stopped at a local pub on his way through town. After listening to several negative comments made by the bartender and others, he shouted, "What a moron! You should ride that mayor out of town on a rail!" Immediately the bartender grabbed him by the throat and threw him over a table. Then 3 other gentlemen took turns punching him in the nose until one of them threw him out the front door!

Another visitor, seated in the corner couldn't contain himself. "I have a question," he exclaimed, "If you guys hate your mayor so much, why did you hit that guy for calling him a Moron?" "He may be a Moron," they answered, "But he's OUR Moron!"

Over the years, I've watched couples fight over parents, friends, and other family members. For example, a husband makes a snide remark about his mother-in-law and instantly, the battle begins as his wife defends her mother, etc. Ironically, when speaking to her privately, the wife often ADMITS that what was said about Momma was true. In other words, "She may be a bad Mom…but she's MY Mom!"

My point isn't to defend insults hurled at each other's parents. Not at all! On the other hand, the sensitivity and instinctive need to defend our own parents illustrates an element of crucified living that is often missing.

That element is best explained by turning to the Bible. In Genesis 2:24 we read, *"That is why a man leaves his father and mother and is united to his wife, and they become one flesh."* In the KJV, it reads "leaves" and "cleave to his wife" or as the old timers like to put it, "Leave and cleave." I remember my pastoral premarital counseling including some instruction about the importance of creating a new home and not clinging to or running to one's parents after marriage. There's a healthy cutting of ties, not completely, but in the sense of priority.

When this doesn't happen, problems result. When couples DO "leave and cleave," the focus is now on the new home and family such that it becomes less likely to feel pulled backwards by the parents or siblings. When conflict or tension exists with the "in-laws" (or "outlaws"), couples who've done it right are able to stand together and not be divided by their families of origin.

Clearly, sacrificing one's parents in lieu of a new home seems like a counter-intuitive foundation to build on. Still, it's a biblical concept. Again, I'm not talking about dishonoring or becoming estranged from our parents or family. What I'm saying is that they no longer get first place and are to be treated as equals to our spouse's family members by both husband and wife.

One of the things we lose in our individualistic western culture is the value of truly getting to know our prospective spouses' family. This is important since, under pressure, we often instinctively revert to what we know. No matter how much we may dislike the way our parents handled conflict or how they communicated for instance, we're likely to handle things the same way when we're stressed. If our spouse knows what our parents and family are like, two benefits result:

1. Our fiancé can make an informed choice based on what life might be like at times should we marry.

2. After marriage, our spouse can help us avoid reverting to negative patterns since they have seen them and understand their context.

To help with this, Prepare-Enrich utilizes the Couple and Family Map.14 The couple map shows how each partner views their current relationship in two areas: flexibility and closeness. The Family Map does the same with each partner's family of origin. Seeing both of these charts together can sometimes be an indicator of what each partner might be likely to do under duress. For example, while a couple may have a good balance of time together versus time alone now, looking at the husband's family of origin might indicate that he will "hide in his man cave" when times get tough.

So while separating from family in terms of autonomy as a couple or authority for decision-making and unity between husband and wife may be a good thing; relationally, we need to know our spouses family of origin and connect with them together.

My wife Karen and I have been married over 30 years. When my parents first got to know Karen, I remember that they just adored her. At one point, my father took me aside and said, "Don't blow this one!" I started to think they liked her more than me! Seriously, later in life, while my wife definitely maintained independence regarding our home, her kitchen, and the responsibility for raising our two children, she truly saw and treated my parents like her own, showing no favoritism. She truly is my role model in this regard.

What about Friends?

Friends too, need to be treated the same way. Frankly, we need to sacrifice all friends who won't sacrifice themselves. What I mean is, any friend who thinks they have a right to pull us away from our spouse or come between us, needs to go. A good friend does all he/she can to support our marriage and help us draw closer. Good friends aren't his friend or her friend alone—they are OUR friends. That isn't to say that a man's male friends or a woman's female friends are going to spend equal time alone with their partner (not a good idea). Rather, they support and value husband and wife and speak into and schedule time to improve their friend's marriage—seeing both husband and wife as important parts of their life.

When a friend tries to pull us away from our spouse or supports divisive speech or actions which negatively affect our relationship with our mate, that friend needs to go. As hard as that may be, it's the right thing. Sometimes jealousy enters over time with friends. I'd rather lose a friend than lose my family. It doesn't normally come to that, but it can. If you need to choose, choose your marriage!

I'd be remiss at this point if I didn't address friends of the opposite sex. I know several folks who've had platonic and healthy relationships with someone they've never been romantically interested in or attracted to. This is fine. Still, once married, this can cause tension and strain. A sacrificial heart is one that's willing to put some distance between that opposite-sex-friend and yourself to make sure your new husband/wife has peace and knows that he/she is "number one" in your life. It avoids the appearance of evil (adultery) and prevents temptation too.

Having said all this, friends can be a true blessing to a married couple. Building friendships with other couples can help your weather the storms of life and realize that you're "not alone" in your struggles. It is GOOD for men to have other men who are "sounding boards" for frustration, etc. The same is true for women. The point is to be sure that your mate knows that they are your priority. Also, those friends need to know that their value comes in part from their commitment to supporting your marriage, not tearing it apart or encouraging behaviors which are destructive.

Chapter Nine: Is Sacrifice Enabling?

Now let's be honest with one another. After reading the first several chapters of this book, you're probably thinking, "This is crazy. In fact, it's dangerous. If I'm supposed to crucify myself and be sacrificial to my spouse, won't he/she just take advantage of me? Isn't this just Christianized enabling? Won't we end-up worse because of my sacrifice just reinforces the negative behavior and attitudes of my spouse?

The concern is legitimate since, as we've already seen, human nature is innately selfish. There are times when unhealthy relationships form as one partner constantly bends over backwards for the other who is MORE than happy to take advantage or their partner's willingness to give. In families afflicted by alcoholism or drug-abuse, it's common to find an enabling spouse who makes matters worse by giving money to the addicted partner or by "covering" for him/her, smoothing-over the circumstances, making excuses, etc.

I remember one couple in particular who could have been "poster children" for this problem. The wife had called me to request help with her husband's alcoholism. I scheduled an appointment to meet with them both. Since I knew her through church, but had never met him, I focused my attention on him during my first visit. As I was talking with him about his addiction, he turned to her and asked for money to buy booze. Before I could react as I was still in shock, she reached in her purse and handed him $20. It was the most blatant example of enabling I had ever witnessed! She hated his drinking and asked her pastor to help him stop. Then, right in front of me, she gave him money for whiskey! Are you kidding me?!!

So how do we avoid enabling while being sacrificial in our relationships?

First, we trust God. In my experience, its one in a hundred couples where the primary problem is that one partner has become a doormat for the other. Honestly, joint selfishness is FAR more common. Thus, to take that first step toward becoming a "Crucified Couple," each of us must trust God to give to us, when we give to our spouse.

Next, in order to avoid enabling, we must understand the difference between enabling and what I call sacrificial service. The key to distinguishing between these two things is to consider what's truly good for your partner. Using my extreme couple example above, was giving her husband $20 for Whiskey "good" for him? Of course not! Thus, saying "No" to him would have been sacrificial. This is especially true when we consider the backlash which would have no-doubt come from him if she stood her ground in refusing to hand him cash!

It's important to understand that sacrificial living in marriage doesn't always involve giving our mate everything he/she wants. Rather, it involves giving our mate what he/she needs. Furthermore, even when giving our spouse what they want, we are to always consider whether or not this will do our partner harm! Will this always be well received? No. Still, we trust God that even in those times, He "has our back" and will bless us.

What does our mate need? Love, respect, honesty, compassion, patience, etc. He/she needs basics like food, clothing and shelter. He/she needs affection and communication too. Wants on the other hand might be a new car or a bigger house or money to spend on lottery tickets or junk food. Giving in to wants might hurt our spouse, no matter what he/she says.

How do you know when to say, "Yes" and when to say, "No?" Beyond the discussion of needs versus wants, the answer to this is based on the fruit. If saying "Yes" produces good results, we probably want to continue. If it produces selfishness and/or abuse, it's time to change that response. This leads to an even bigger discussion, how do we know when our approach is working in general? We'll deal with this in the next chapter.

Chapter Ten: Defining Success...
"How Will I Know it's Working?"

Years ago, I came across a book that I've recommended to couples ever since. The book is called, <u>Divorce Busting</u> and it's by Marilyn Weiner-Davis.15 I also recommend her website, <u>www.divorce-busting.com</u>. What do I love about it?

Well, for one thing, Ms. Davis deals with the question, "What can I do if my spouse won't cooperate?" Her book contains a series of case studies. Most are cases where one partner came to Ms. Davis for counseling, but their spouse refused. In each case, she discussed how changes they might make would influence the environment in their home regardless of whether or not their partner was even aware of what was changing or why. In each case, positive change occurred in the relationship, thus the case studies are both informative and encouraging.

Perhaps you find yourself in the same situation as you're reading this book. You want healthy change in your marriage, but your spouse isn't engaged in this process. Perhaps he/she thinks everything is OK. Perhaps they've given up. Perhaps they are depressed and just can't bring themselves to make the effort necessary to change. Whatever the case, <u>Divorce Busting</u> may be helpful.

In the meantime, you still need to know if changes you're making as a result of this book are working so let me make a few suggestions. The first is, give it time. You will no doubt need to consistently live out healthy change for a few months before significant change occurs. Second, don't feel sorry for yourself if you have to take the initiative. This is normally the case. You've heard it said, "It takes two to tango." I agree, but normally one person is the first to ask the other to dance. Third, when you do make changes, I'd suggest you be prepared for the opposite reaction to changes at first. It's not unusual for a spouse to respond negatively to even positive changes.

Why?

One reason is that human beings often hate change in general. To many people, change is just unsettling, thus unattractive. Also, I believe there's a subconscious instinctive reaction to positive change whereby we try to "poke holes in it," to see if the change is real and permanent. This is especially true if we've been "burned" before. Our fear is that the change might not last or might be a false show. So, rather than get our hopes up, we attack the change or the person making the change. If they respond in anger, we conclude that the change isn't real or lasting.

If your spouse responds negatively to the things you're trying to do, evaluate them based on God's Word and Will. If they are truly good things and demonstrate love and concern for your spouse, don't quit just because your mate is grouchy or angry about the change. If your spouse tries to make fun of the change or accuse you of being disingenuous, just double-down and keep going. After a few weeks, the ice may melt and positive response may be the result.

I remember a friend of mine going through this with his wife. He had been working too hard and not communicating well with her. She stopped talking to him and seemed to be inclined to leave. He woke her up in the middle of the night (not something I'd recommend) and told her, "I know you won't believe me, but I'm going to make some changes and I want you to know that I love you."

For the first several weeks she made fun of him when he'd try to talk to her. When he took time off to be at home, she'd scoff and say that she "wasn't going to fall for it." Still, after he continued undaunted, she eventually came up to him, hugged him, and apologized for being so mean. Today, they are a very happy couple.

Eventually, the goal is for joint and mutual sacrifice. Ultimately, you want to see both partners making healthy changes. This creates a multiplication effect where a "perfect storm" of positive change and healthy patterns appear. I normally suggest that couples retake the Prepare-Enrich inventory mentioned earlier to see how things have advanced in the 10 major relationship categories measured by that system. The original inventory provides a benchmark to measure against over time. Another option is "Couple Checkup," found at https://www.couplecheckup.com. This is a self-directed inventory couples can use at any time to measure the health of their relationship and to see how it's changing.

Still, we need to discuss what to do if nothing ultimately improves or if things get worse. What about separation? Divorce? Ongoing counseling or medication? Let's consider these things and more in chapter 11.

Chapter Eleven: Separation and Divorce…Cause or Cure?

Over the years, I've been amazed at how often I've encountered couples and even a few Christian Counselors who treat separation as a potential remedy or alternative to divorce. Some even see it as a virtual sure-fire cure. My experience has been that, despite the old cliché, absence normally doesn't make "the heart grow fonder!"

In many cases, a prolonged separation just makes divorce easier since it seems to be less unsettling, sort-of the next logical step. So if you goal is divorce, separation may help you get there in a more gradual, less shocking way. Still, as a pastor, my goal is not to see more divorces and most couple I've married didn't walk down the aisle thinking about how they might get divorced in a few years!

Sometimes, there are helpful and less divisive options to consider in lieu of a prolonged or legal separation. Having a night or two weekly when each partner goes out with their friends (of the same gender) can take some of the tension off if both are in agreement to grant this "extra space." Another option is to take a personal spiritual retreat to regroup, draw close to God and reboot. Of course doing the "Prepare-Enrich" counseling program mentioned earlier in this book can help as well.

Having said this, there are times when separation may be the only reasonable step. In the case of physical abuse for instance, I always recommend a season of separation while the abuser seeks treatment and demonstrates the fruit of change. If the fighting and screaming is increasing out of control and small children are at home, I may recommend a short period of separation while we teach and practice conflict resolution techniques, etc.

Even if separation is necessary, there is a right way and a wrong way to go about it. Here are some "dos and don'ts" to consider:

1. DO set a limit on the separation. This may not be an exact timeframe, but there should be an "end game." In the case of abuse for instance, if the abuser gets counseling, demonstrates a pattern of healthy anger management for 3 months, and the couple "dates" for 3 months more, a trial over night and then reconciliation will be attempted. This gives both partners peace and restates the objective to be together as opposed to seeing separation is just the first step toward an inevitable divorce.

2. DON'T cheat. If you say you're going to separate for a month and then try coming back together, don't wait a week and then move back in. Why not? Because if things TRULY were bad enough to warrant this month-long time-out, you should take advantage of it and use it productively.

3. DO seek counsel. Don't do divorce in a vacuum. Separation is a time to work on yourself and prepare to

sacrifice for and bless your spouse. It is not a time to stay home alone and pout. Nor is it a time to find your relationship-challenged friends so they can tell you to get divorced and then plan a wild trip to Las Vegas. Listen to God during this time and get wise counsel from others who do the same!

4. Don't talk about divorce during this time. Believe in the benefits of what you're doing and look forward to reconciliation. Remember how you loved one another in the past. Look forward to more of the same.

Crucified Divorce?

This brings me to a difficult topic. The question is, can divorce be sacrificial? Sadly, my answer is, "Sometimes, yes." I remember years ago attempting to do an intervention with a troubled family. Mom was a heavy drinker and Dad was at his wits end. I suggested an intervention with all the kids involved. Unfortunately, some of the kids objected and Dad decided not to pursue the intervention. Mom ultimately drank herself to death. Her funeral was one of the most difficult I've ever had to do.

One of the reasons this intervention was so difficult for the family was that they were preparing to say, "You choose—either you reject the bottle and get help or you're rejecting us. If you don't stop drinking, you're out of our lives!" Tough talk, but experts say it's often necessary in order for the seriousness of the problem to be understood such that corrective action is taken. The husband's responsibility in this scenario would have been to pursue separation and perhaps divorce had she not complied. How is this sacrificial? First, it hurts! It's hard! It's expensive too!

But need it have been final?

More than once in my ministry, I've seen someone take a stand in divorce which resulted in repentance and change in their partner. The sacrifice of taking this stand resulted in change and blessing! Again, this is rare, but something that at times makes sense.

Lest you write me letters showing that God hates divorce, let me say that I agree. Still, what did God say about Israel after years of her rebellion? Notice Jer. 3:8, *"I gave faithless Israel her certificate of divorce and sent her away because of all her adulteries. Yet I saw that her unfaithful sister Judah had no fear; she also went out and committed adultery."*

The real question is, to coin a phrase, "When does the fat lady sing?" Furthermore, I'd ask, "Does she do encores?" Is there a time for divorce? Yes. Having said that, is it necessarily final? No!! In fact, I Corinthians 7:10-11 suggests that remaining single even in this case is often a precursor to reconciliation. My intent here isn't to do a biblical exegesis with regard to divorce and/or remarriage. Normally as a pastor, I don't utter "the D word" in counseling situations, nor do I encourage couples to even discuss it. Still, in cases where health and safety is concerned, divorce can be a sacrificial choice to force change as a last resort. God's example with Israel is an example. Understanding the Church as spiritual Israel and Gentiles as grafted members of Israel as in the book of Galatians, we may even see the marriage of the lamb in Revelation 19 as the ultimate reconciliation following God's divorce of Israel.

While I believe in two biblical exceptions whereby divorce and then a remarriage to a new partner is allowed—even for Christians, I see these as just that—exceptions! God's norm is to marry for life. Can repeated sexual sin or the departure of a non-Christian spouse be grounds for divorce and remarriage? Yes. Still, as we've already seen, it's God's desire for us to reconcile even in these extreme cases.

In these extreme and often difficult cases, couples often need outside help. Frankly, some of these may require counseling and assistance from someone trained beyond the discipline of pastoral care. What, where, and when should you seek that help? We'll look at that next.

Chapter Twelve: Getting Help—If this book doesn't help, then what?

As a pastor and an author, I'm a realist. I read once that people forget 75% of what they hear within 48 hours. Actually, I proved this once with one of my own sermons. I used to write sermons and then a small group discussion outline (like the Discussion Questions for Couples in the appendix of this book). One week I was visiting a small group study just a couple of days after preaching the sermon based on the outline I had written. The first question was, "Name one thing you remember and were encouraged by from last week's sermon." As a joke, the small group leader called on me with that question. I drew a complete blank. After writing the sermon, giving the sermon, and writing the small group discussion outline; I couldn't even recall the topic!

So if this is true even for authors, how much more for those of you reading this book. The only way you'll remember and benefit from any of it is to use it and apply it until it becomes "second nature." I encourage you to do the discussion questions and maybe even form a couples group to read and talk these things through together.

Even with all of that, I'm sure some may need more. While my wife and I are often able to help many couples who struggle, there are times when we encounter folks with issues needing help "far above our pay grade." What then?

First, let me recommend again Prepare-Enrich. I have never encountered a more thorough program. First, the inventory gives you a sense of what strengths and growth areas you have as a couple based on 10-12 primary relationship categories such as communication, conflict resolution, sexual relationship, finances, etc. Next, the accompanying workbook contains literally dozens of exercises to help build skills and improve in areas of weakness. Prepare-Enrich has been tested across multiple racial, age, national, language, and socio- economic groups and found extremely accurate and helpful as a tool to strengthen relationships.

I'd also recommend Dr. Neil Anderson's "Steps to Freedom in Christ."16 This 7 step prayer process can help with issues such as forgiveness and truly engage Jesus as the one who breaks the bondage of sin and selfishness that cripples couples. My wife and I have helped dozens of couples with both this and the Prepare-Enrich program. We use the Prepare-Enrich program, Neil Anderson's material, plus the information in this book to help couples either in person or via. Skype, Gotomeeting, or phone conferencing service. The cost is $250 per couple and it includes a workbook, couples inventory report, a copy of this book, and three live sessions with one or both of us. If you'd like to work with us online and/or by phone, please call (860) 938-2725 or email me at JoelRissinger@johnmaxwellgroup.com

Finally, a word about Christian Counselors. Like anything else, there are good ones and bad ones. Some who claim to be Christian Counselors are nothing but Freudian secular practitioners who add a few verses and throw-out Jesus' name here and there. In my experience, counselors either come from a Christian perspective or they don't. If they do, they understand that we are sinners by nature and need Jesus to forgive and change us. If they do not have a Christian worldview, they are simply looking for a way to "get rid of the rough edges" and have us live-out what they believe to be our innate goodness. This is ultimately disastrous.

The best way to find a good Christian counselor is to call 3-4 solid evangelical churches in your area and ask them for a referral to a licensed counselor who they know to be a believer. Short of that, the American Association of Christian Counselors, AACC, may also be helpful.17

My final word to you however, would be this: Don't Quit!

Remember that famous poem by Edger A. Guest?[18]

Don't Quit!

When things go wrong, as they sometimes will,

When the road you're trudging seems all uphill,
When the funds are low and the debts are high,
And you want to smile, but you have to sigh,
When care is pressing you down a bit-
Rest if you must, but don't you quit.

Life is queer with its twists and turns,

As every one of us sometimes learns,
And many a fellow turns about
When he might have won had he stuck it out.
Don't give up though the pace seems slow -
You may succeed with another blow.

Often the goal is nearer than

It seems to a faint and faltering man;
Often the struggler has given up
When he might have captured the victor's cup;
And he learned too late when the night came down,
How close he was to the golden crown.

Success is failure turned inside out -

The silver tint in the clouds of doubt,

And you never can tell how close you are,
It might be near when it seems afar;
So stick to the fight when you're hardest hit -
It's when things seem worst that you must not quit.15

I think the thing that I bring to most couples who may be struggling is that if both of you want to make things work, you can. I've seen it all…couples who've come to me after one has filed for divorce and the other is in an ongoing adulterous affair, etc. I've witnessed several of those come back together and live a long and happy life together after healing. Far too many give up too soon. Please don't! Get help. Pray. And work through your issues. Things can and will improve. I truly believe that…

My prayer is that you will believe it too!

Discussion Questions for Groups and Couples

NOTE: These questions are intended to be used by a couple or in a small group setting after reading each chapter. Use them as a primer for ongoing conversation, learning, and growth.

CHAPTER ONE: The Death of Death to Self

1. How, if at all, did this chapter challenge your worldview?

2. How does our self-focused culture affect your relationship as a couple?

3. How can you help your children capture the idea of dying to self?

4. What is one practical way you can love sacrificially today?

CHAPTER TWO: The Key to Marriage—Sacrifice.

1. How do you think your marriage is like Christ and the Church? How is it different?

2. Does your Church help your marriage? If not, what can you do to help change that?

3. What is the hardest thing for you to sacrifice or give up, to help your marriage?

CHAPTER THREE: Sacrificial Communication.
1. How would you characterize the communication in your relationship? How is it good? How could it be better?
2. What IS good communication? Bad communication?
3. What are the barriers to good communication?
4. How can you be a better listener? How can you be assertive without being offensive?

CHAPTER FOUR: Sacrificial Conflict Resolution

1. What is your typical experience when attempting to resolve conflict? What works? What doesn't?

2. Which of the 10 steps in this chapter will be the hardest for you? Why? Are you willing to sacrifice in this area?

3. How do the communication techniques in Chapter Three affect conflict resolution?

4. How can good conflict resolution strategies help you in other relationships at work, in school, etc.?

CHAPTER FIVE: Dying to your budget.

1. As a couple, how are you the same regarding the use of money? How are you different?

2. Why do you think money trouble is one of the most common reasons for divorce? What does that say about our culture?

3. What changes can each of you make to "die" to yourself when budgeting?

4. How would applying the principles in this chapter help your family?

CHAPTER SIX: Sacrificial Sex.

1. As with money, sex one of the primary reasons for marital failure. Why do think this is true?

2. Why don't couples communicate better about sex such that differences in this department can be resolved? How might you learn to communicate better regarding sexual likes or dislikes?

3. How has the "sexual revolution" of the 1960's affected marriages? Do you think it has had an impact on you?

4. How, if at all, does affection differ from sex? Does your interest in these things differ from your spouse? If so, how do you sacrifice for him/her to help compensate for this difference?

CHAPTER SEVEN: Crucified Fun Times.

1. What fun things do you do as a couple?

2. What fun things/activities would you like to try as a couple?

3. Why do you think leisure activities are so important in marriage?

4. If your interests differ from your spouses, what things are you willing to do with him/her regardless of that difference?

CHAPTER EIGHT: Family and Friends…letting go!

1. Have family and/or friends ever caused stress in your marriage? How did you handle that?

2. Is it hard for you to keep your spouse in "first place," such that family and friends can't interfere in your relationship?

3. If you were counseling a young couple preparing for marriage, how would you explain the principle of "leave and cleave?"

CHAPTER NINE: Is sacrifice enabling?

1. How do you distinguish between saying "Yes" out of sacrifice versus enabling sinful/harmful behavior in your partner? When is saying "No" to your spouse an act of sacrifice?

2. When does God say, "No" to us? Is this cruel?

3. How do you determine when to say "No" to your children? Is the principle at work any different than re. your spouse?

CHAPTER TEN: Defining Success.

1. How do you define success in marriage? Does this differ from your spouse's definition?

2. What do you think is the hardest thing to change to achieve success in marriage? Are you willing to make that change?

3. What would you like your great-grandchildren to say about you a couple?

CHAPTER ELEVEN: Separation and Divorce.

1. Why do you think 50% of marriages end in divorce? Do you think separation is a contributing factor to this statistic?

2. What is the impact of divorce on children? Are you willing to personally make changes to protect your children from this?

3. What are you willing to do for your spouse without being asked? Will you do this for them today?

CHAPTER TWELVE: Getting Help.

1. In addition to the resources listed in this chapter, what are some good books or tools you think can help a struggling couple?

2. Do you personally like receiving counsel/seeing a therapist? Why or why not? Is this something you'd like to do for your marriage?

3. Is asking for help hard for you or your spouse? Are you sacrificially willing to do it anyway?

Sample budget.

Flintstone Monthly Family Budget (Dec 2014)

INCOME: (Estimate)

Source		Amount (Net)
Fred's Salary		$_____
Fred's 2nd Job		$_____
Wilma's Salary	$	$_____
Other Income	+	$_____
Total:		$

EXPENSES:

Item	**Amount**
	Due
Offerings/Charity--	$
Mortgage--	$
Car Payments--	$
Student Loans--	$
Food--	$
Gas & Tolls--	$
Electricity--	$
Heat/Oil--	$*
Water Bill--	$
Cell Phone --	$
AAA Auto--	$
Cable/Other Utilities-	$
DMV--	$*
Car Repairs--	$*

Vet--	$*
Other Taxes (Car, Prop.)-	$*
Invest Life Insurance	$
Home Repairs--	$*
Mowing/Snow--	$*
Medical--	$*
Clothing--	$*
Bank Fees--	$
Vitamins--	$
Entertainment--	$
Pay Loans--	$
Gifts*--	$*
Misc.—	$*
TOTAL:	$ (Should match income total above)

*=Saved till needed.

Footnotes

1. Hawkins, Dr. Alan, *Should I Keep Trying to Work it Out?*, *(Report produced on behalf of the Utah Commission on Marriage, Salt Lake City, UT, October 2009), page 41.*

2. Joel L. Rissinger, *The Crucified Church,* (Newington, CT, Xulon Elite, 2010), pages 32-   33.

3. Ibid., Pages 35-41

4. Ibid, Pages 41-43.

5. Smalley, Gary, "Hidden Keys to Lasting Relationships," (Thomas Nelson, January, 2001).

6. Eggerlichs, Dr. Emmerson, *Love & Respect,* Thomas Nelson; (September 7, 2004), **ISBN-10:** 1591451876

7. Chaplain, Gary D., Northfield Publishing; New Edition edition (January 1, 2010), **ISBN-10:** 0802473156

8. Covey, Stephen, *Seven Habits of Highly Effective People,* **Publisher:** Simon Schuster Ltd Uk; Illustrated. edition (1990), **ISBN-10:** 406204983X

9. Prepare-Enrich, www.prepare-enrich.com.

10. Life Innovations, 10 Steps to Resolving Couple Conflict, www.prepare-enrich.com.

11. Campbell, David P., *If You Don't Know Where You're Going, You'll Probably End-up Somewhere Else,* Thomas More Association (July 1990), **ISBN-10:** 0883473275

12. Ramsey, David, *Total Money Makeover,* Thomas Nelson; First Edition edition (September 11, 2003) **ISBN-10:** 0785263268

13. Yellen, Pamela, *Bank on Yourself,* (New York, NY), Vanguard Press, 2009.

14. Prepare-Enrich, Couple and Family Map, www.prepare-enrich.com.

15. Davis, Marilyn Weiner-Davis, *Divorce Busting,* A Fireside Book; Reprint edition (February 1, 1993), **ISBN-10:** 0671797255.

16. Anderson, Neil, *The Bondage Breaker,* Harvest House Publishers; 1 edition (December 15, 2006) **ISBN-10:** 0736918140.

17. American Association of Christian Counselors, www.aacc.net.

18. Guest, Edgar A., "Don't Quit," www.thedontquitpoem.com.

Recommended Reading

Rainer, Thom S., Eric Geiger. *Simple Church, B&H Publishing Group, 2006, ISBN 0805443908.*

Davis, Marilyn-Weiner, *Divorce Busting,* A Fireside Book; Reprint edition (February 1, 1993), **ISBN-10:** 0671797255.

Rissinger, Joel, *The Crucified Church,* Xulon Publishing, 2010, ISBN 9781609578046.

Smalley, Gary, *Love is a Decision,* Thomas Nelson (January 1, 2001), **ISBN-10:** 0849942683.

Ramsey, Dave, *Total Money Makeover,* Thomas Nelson; First Edition ,(September 11, 2003), **ISBN-10:** 0785263268

Cymbala, Jim, Merrill, Dean. *Fresh Wind, Fresh Fire.* Zondervan 2003, ISBN 0310251532

Olson, David T., The American Church in Crisis, Tyndale, 2005. ISBN 13:978-0-310-27713-2

Hybels, Bill, Mittleberg, Mark, Strobel, Lee. *The Contagious Christian,* Zondervan, 2007,ISBN 0310257875

Colson, Chuck, Pearcey, Nancy. *The Christian in Today's Culture: Developing a Biblical Worldview,* Tyndale, 2001, ISBN 0842355871

Anderson, Neil, *The Bondage Breaker,* Harvest House Publishers; 1 edition (December 15, 2006) **ISBN-10:** 0736918140.

Yellen, Pamela, *Bank on Yourself,* New York, NY, Vanguard Press, 2009, ISBN 978-59315-496-7

About the Author

Pastor Joel L. Rissinger and his wife Karen have been married for more than 30 years and have two adult children, a marvelous son-in-law, and one gorgeous granddaughter. Pastor Joel is the lead and founding pastor of Mill Pond Church in Newington, Connecticut. Mill Pond started with fifteen people, mostly teens, in the Rissinger's living room in the summer of 2006. Today, Mill Pond is an established, thriving church actively helping other churches launch.

Pastor Joel has been in fulltime ministry since 1992. In this capacity, he has led several congregations through major transitions prior to planting Mill Pond Church. He and his wife Karen, a School Psychologist have helped hundreds of couples through counseling, their popular "Marriage Time-Out" retreats, Iron Sharpens Iron Seminars, and other public ministry.

In addition to his pastoral duties, Pastor Joel is a Certified Speaker, Trainer and Coach with the John Maxwell Group. Joel speaks in corporate, non-profit, and civic group settings on a regular basis and is also a leader with Marketplace Chaplains, where he manages Chaplains serving employees and married couples throughout Central CT. In the recent past, Joel served as a presenter for the "Perspectives" Missions course, and as a seminar presenter for Life Innovations, Inc., and their popular Prepare-Enrich marriage counseling program. He is also a graduate of the famous "Bill Gove Speech Workshop."

Pastor Joel has a BA in theology from Ambassador University, as well as MAs in both religion and religious education from Liberty University. He is currently a D.Min. student with the Antioch School in Ames, Iowa. Karen Rissinger has her BA in Theology also from Ambassador as well as a Masters in School Psychology from the University of Hartford, CT.

Made in the USA
Middletown, DE
02 September 2016